■K 24 HOURS
Mountain

LONDON, NEW YORK, MUNICH,
MELBOURNE, and DELHI

Written and edited by Fleur Star
Designed by Karen Hood

Art Director Rachael Foster
Publishing Manager Susan Leonard
Category Publisher Mary Ling

Picture Researcher Jo Walton
Production Controller Lucy Baker
DTP Designers Almudena Díaz,
Emma Hansen-Knarhoi
Jacket Designer Hedi Gutt

Consultant Kerstin Swahn

First published in Great Britain in 2007 by
Dorling Kindersley Limited
80 Strand, London WC2R 0RL

Copyright © 2007 Dorling Kindersley Limited
A Penguin Company

2 4 6 8 10 9 7 5 3 1
AD304 – 10/06

A CIP catalogue record for this book
is available from the British Library.

ISBN 978-1-40531-623-1

Colour reproduction by Colourscan, Singapore
Printed and bound by
L. Rex Printing Co. Ltd, China

Discover more at
www.dk.com

Welcome to the Andes,

6:00 am Dawn

10:00 am Morning

A mountain is a harsh environment, yet
many animals thrive up on the slopes. Spend
24 hours with some of them and discover how
they eat, sleep, and survive on the tough terrain.

the longest **mountain range** in the world.

`2:00 pm` **Afternoon**

`6:00 pm` **Dusk**

`10:00 pm` **Night**

Lakes are typically found in a central Andean region called the Altiplano. There are also dry grasslands here, called puna. The lusher grasslands found in the north are called paramo.

In *24 Hours Mountain* we spend a day and night in the Andes to look at the creatures that live up above the tree line. During the 24 hours, we return to the five animals shown on this page to see what they are doing.

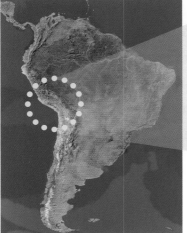

The Andes runs down the whole of the west coast of South America.

This book is set in the Altiplano region of the central Andes and on the paramo grasslands to the north.

Puma

Also called mountain lions or cougars, pumas can be found all over the Andes. They live and hunt alone, apart from mothers with their cubs.

Culpeo

The culpeo is also called the Andean red fox, but its red fur only develops as an adult. The cubs are sandy coloured, which is good camouflage against predators.

Andean condor

The world's largest birds of prey, these condors also have the biggest wingspan of any bird. But they have no voice boxes, so their call sounds like a cough.

Vicuña

Vicuñas are related to llamas. They are the "camels" of the Andes, able to cope well in extreme conditions found at great heights.

Scale Look out for scale guides as you read through the book to help you work out the size of the creatures you meet. They are based on children 115 cm (3 ft 9 in) tall.

The changing seasons

Dry Between April and October, the sun and wind dry the surface of the salt lakes in the Altiplano, leaving a 60 cm- (2 ft-) thick crust of salt on top of the water.

Rainy Even when the salt lakes begin to fill, shallow water at the edge of the lakes evaporates. The region can flood to 2 m (6 ft) deep.

Spectacled bear

The only bears to be found in South America, spectacled bears live in cloud forests and lush grasslands (called paramo).

1 Guanaco

A lone guanaco stands in the cold morning air, watching the Sun rise over the Andes. By the time the Sun has emerged over the mountain peaks, the sunrise can seem later than it actually is.

A herd of **vicuñas** makes its way down from its sleeping area high up in the mountains. The lower slopes provide lusher grass for grazing.

Spectacled bears are most active at dawn and dusk, heading up the slopes to the grasslands to feed on their favourite food: puya plants.

The nocturnal **culpeo** breakfasts on a carcass. It usually hunts small animals such as rodents and lizards, but is happy to scavenge a free meal.

Before **Andean condors** take flight in the morning, they stretch out their wings to dry their feathers, which are wet with dawn dew.

A **puma** sniffs the air, picking up the smell of another puma's urine. The cats scent-mark their territories to stop others getting too close.

High up in the mountains, where it is too cold for trees to grow, many animals battle the biting winds and strong sunlight to graze the grasslands. The lusher grasses of the paramo provide better fodder than the drier, sparser puna to the south.

Like many deer, huemals "drop antlers" every year. They "come into velvet" – grow new antlers – in time for the mating season.

Male huemals use their antlers to fight over mates.

Huemals, which are also called Andean deer, are typical herbivores. They easily climb the rocky slopes to find plants, but they are not built to fight predators. Instead, they run at high speeds to escape.

Tapirs fight over mates and territory by **biting**.

Mountain tapirs divide their day between rivers and paramo, where the solitary, aggressive animals hide in the grasses. When threatened, tapirs may hide from their attackers in a river. They can stay underwater for several minutes, using their snouts as snorkels.

A wagging white tail is a sign that the deer is afraid.

White-tailed deer make hours-long foraging trips at dawn and dusk. If a fawn is too young to keep up, its mother hides it among the vegetation.

The plants of the paramo

– many of which don't grow anywhere else – attract lots of birds, which feed on their nectar and the insects that pollinate them.

Hummingbirds like to feed from the 12 m- (40 ft-) tall *Puya ramondii* herb.

Andean hillstars, like other hummingbirds, survive the cold nights by going into torpor – they lower their body temperatures to one-third of their daytime level to save energy.

Andean flickers are woodpeckers – birds that are most famous for hammering their bills into tree trunks. But there are no trees on the paramo, only shrubs and smaller plants, so the flicker picks insects off the rocks to eat.

Bearded helmetcrest hummingbirds prefer walking to flying in their search for food, as they eat insects rather than nectar. The bird gets its name from the crest that makes its head appear twice its real size!

Caracaras are small birds of prey. They patrol the paramo in groups, looking for carcasses to scavenge, and also eating insects and snails.

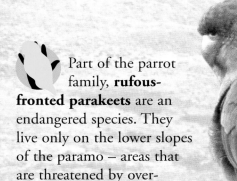

Part of the parrot family, **rufous-fronted parakeets** are an endangered species. They live only on the lower slopes of the paramo – areas that are threatened by over-grazing and farming.

Seedsnipes don't build nests, but dig shallow scrapes on the ground to lay their eggs in, which they sit on for about four weeks until they hatch. The chicks are able to walk and eat right away.

To the south of the paramo, an Andean hairy armadillo wanders over the barren puna. Sniffing out an **insect**, it unearths the food with a scrape of its long, sharp **claws**.

Twenty bony plates cover the armadillo's body. Hair grows between the plates, keeping the animal warm.

On the menu

Armadillos are omnivores: they'll eat anything from plants to rodents.

Insects such as beetles are nourishing snacks, but they are not very filling.

Armadillos will dig under and even into rotting carcasses to get at juicy maggots.

The armadillo is only active in the daytime during winter. Summer heat forces it to turn its day around, searching for food at night and spending the day in cool burrows.

Armadillos live alone, only sharing burrows with their young.

The word "armadillo" means little plated one.

Strong claws make fast work of digging a 3 m- (10 ft-) deep burrow. The holes are not used more than once.

The best place to hide from predators is underground, but when there's no burrow to dive into, the armadillo covers its legs and relies on its armour plating.

1 Juvenile Andean condor
2 Adult male Andean condor

J**ust as** there are high peaks in mountainous territory, there are also deep valleys. Colca Canyon is thought to be the world's deepest gorge (narrow valley). The steep slopes are a favoured roosting site for Andean condors.

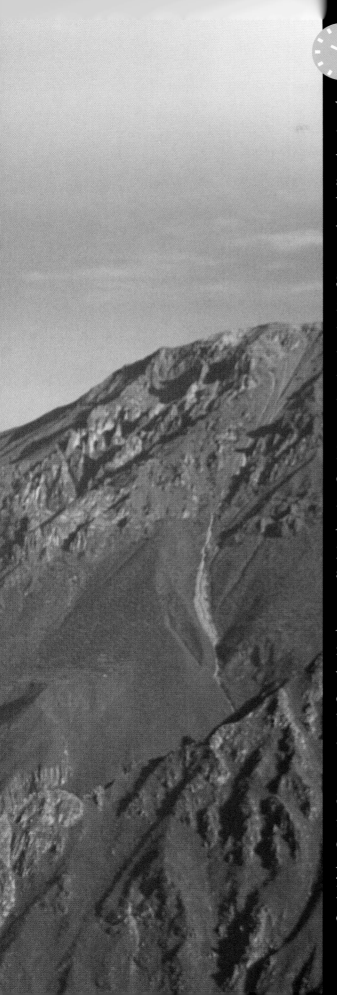

Vicuñas are grazers: their day is taken up with eating, drinking, and chewing the cud. Young vicuñas even eat while lying down.

Spectacled bears live in cloud forests below the grasslands. During the day, they rest in the trees, bending branches to make "nests" to sit in.

Fully fed, the nocturnal **culpeo** settles down to rest among the rocks. An adult culpeo has few predators, so it is safe to sleep out in the open.

An **Andean condor** finds a dead vicuña: this will be its first meal for days. Its strong, hooked bill easily tears through the decaying flesh.

Solitary **pumas** spend their daytime asleep. Only mothers with young cubs are still out hunting to keep their offspring well fed.

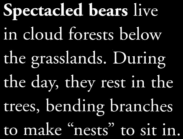

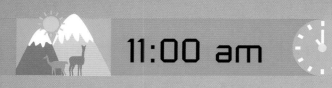

There's competition in the air between the birds of prey that live around the Andes. Scavenging turkey vultures sniffing out a carcass are sometimes followed by condors, which chase them off the food.

The condor's large wingspan allows it to glide for hundreds of kilometres (miles).

All birds rely on their feathers for flight. They cannot fly if feathers are bent or damaged.

Turkey vultures have weak **claws** because they do not need to kill for food.

Turkey vultures are the only birds with a good sense of smell, which is useful for tracking down dead animals through tall grasses and shrubs.

Condors have excellent eyesight, able to see dead animals and even birds' eggs on the ground while soaring high above them. They fly 320 km (200 miles) a day looking for food.

With an outstretched neck that makes him stand up straight, a male condor raises his wings in a courtship display, trying to attract a mate. The bird hisses and clucks for female attention.

The condor rides air currents to gain height. It rises almost 1 km (0.6 miles) in just two minutes.

A flying start

11:30 am Peregrine falcons lay their eggs in a shallow nest, called a scrape, right on the edge of the mountainside.

You need to be quick to spot a **peregrine falcon**: they are among the world's fastest birds. They can reach 230 km/h (145 mph) diving for prey, which they kill with their sharp bills.

30 days later The chicks have hatched, and just seven weeks later they will learn to fly – a dangerous task at the top of a mountain.

4 months later The chicks have survived flying lessons, but still rely on both parents to bring them food: other birds.

Condors are scavengers:

they feed on animals that are already **dead**, but they might also attack young or dying animals. Despite feeding in **flocks**, it can take them days to finish a large carcass.

Bald head for poking inside carcass without getting feathers mucky.

Sharp, hooked bill for gripping prey and ripping into flesh.

First come, first served
The birds gather round the day's meal in a strict pecking order. Males eat first; they are bigger than the females and perform displays to frighten off other scavengers that might be around. They rarely fight, because that could damage their feathers.

Having gorged itself on guanaco, this young condor waits for a thermal (air current) to carry it into flight. It has eaten too much to take off itself.

The flock COVERS the carcass.

1 Guanaco

Between the peaks, lakes dot the Altiplano region of the Andes. Some are filled with rain or melted snow; others form from geysers that erupt from below the surface. Many provide drinking water for animals.

Two young **vicuñas** start a play-fight, imitating the adults in the herd. Adult males wrestle each other to take sole control of the herd's females.

Feeling peckish, the **spectacled bear** surveys the forest for a snack. There are plenty of bromeliad plants within arm's reach of its nest.

Young **culpeos** are targets for birds of prey, so the safest place for them to sleep during the day is in an underground burrow with their mother.

The **Andean condor** gets mucky when it feeds, and needs to preen its feathers afterwards. It even rubs its head on the ground to get the blood off.

A female **puma** watches over her three cubs while at rest. The small, young cubs could be targeted as prey by foxes or even other pumas.

There are 41 islands in Lake Titicaca, which is just a little smaller than Cyprus.

The freshwater Lake Titicaca is the world's highest navigable lake (big enough for boats to sail on). Located in the Altiplano, it is home to frogs and fish that don't exist anywhere else in the world.

The Titicaca frog's saggy skin helps it to breathe. Frogs absorb oxygen through their skin, and the bigger the skin, the more oxygen it can absorb.

This is the world's largest frog.

The giant Titicaca frog lives in the shallows of the lake, avoiding roasting in the sun by never leaving the water. Its dark skin also gives protection against the Sun's rays.

Some Titicaca frogs have green skin; others can be dark and spotty.

24

Teams of **neotropic cormorants** work together to get food. They wade through the lake, flapping their wings to chase the fish into shallow water.

The lake teems with **fish**, which **attract** lots of birds.

Argentine silverside fish

Killifish

The **puna ibis** uses its long, curved bill to probe for food in the shallow waters and the mud around the edge of the lake. Groups of ibis feed together, seeking fish, frogs, and small aquatic animals to eat.

Three's a crowd

Three species of flamingos live on the lakes: Andean, Chilean, and Puna. As soon as the birds arrive, they start the search for a mate.

At the start of the rainy season, flocks of flamingos settle on the salt lakes in the Altiplano. The lakes are far smaller than Lake Titicaca, yet thousands of birds feed here.

There's no competition between the three species as they eat different food.

Flamingos turn pink from the carotenoids in the algae or shrimp they eat. It's the same pigment that turns carrots orange.

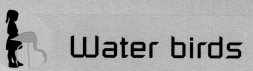

Water birds

Bringing up baby

October Flamingo pairs build their nests, ready for laying a single egg. The lakeside is covered in volcano-shaped mounds of mud.

December The fluffy grey chick has just hatched. The 60 cm- (2 ft-) high nest keeps the bird safe from any flood waters.

April The chick has grown out of its "baby" feathers and is ready to fly, but still relies on its mother for food.

At night, flamingos roost near hot geysers so they do not **freeze**.

Flamingos turn their heads upside-down to eat. They use their bills as sieves, sifting food from the water.

27

There's more to the Altiplano than lakes and puna grassland. The Andes is a chain of volcanoes, many of which are still bubbling away underground. This activity comes to the surface through geysers and pools of boiling mud.

An outgoing geyser

The hot steam cools in the air, condenses into water, and runs into lakes.

4:00 pm The pressure of volcanic activity pushes steam through holes in the ground, making the water in the geyser boil.

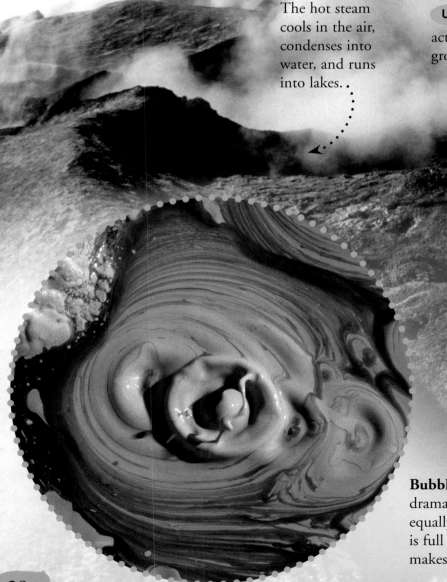

Bubbling mud might not look as dramatic as a geyser, but it has an equally strong presence: the mud is full of sulphur, a mineral that makes the air stink like rotten eggs.

4:01 pm The steam quickly cools and becomes water. Only bacteria and algae can live in the boiling pool, colouring it red and green.

6:10 am As the pressure builds up below ground, the geyser suddenly and briefly erupts, sending a jet of hot water and steam into the air.

Hot days, freezing nights, strong winds, and very little rainfall turns parts of the Altiplano into salt deserts. The salts are minerals found in the ground, brought to the surface in lakes.

Melted snow and water from geysers run down the slopes to form lakes.

Small **iguanid lizards** scamper over the lake's salty crust, catching flies to eat.

1 Guanaco

Sunset falls later in the day the further south you move through the Andes, away from the equator. With light fading as soon as the Sun sinks behind the peaks, there is little time for a guanaco to find a safe place to sleep.

Unlike guanacos, **vicuñas** drink lots of water during the day. They never stray far from rivers or lakes when grazing on the rocky slopes.

The **spectacled bear** leaves its tree to search the forest and paramo for food. Although mostly vegetarian, it will also eat small animals.

The **culpeo** rouses itself from its daytime rest to go hunting. A male culpeo with young cubs needs to get food for his family as well as himself.

Feeding and preening all day must be tiring work for an **Andean condor**! Giving a huge yawn, it prepares to return to its roost for the night.

From a high point on the peaks, the **puma** scans the mountains for prey. It prefers large deer or guanaco, but any meat will do.

With its thick fur, grooming is an important part of viscacha hair-care! ...

Viscachas have many predators,

Perched on a rock, a male viscacha watches for predators while his colony feeds. At the first sign of danger, he will call out a warning.

A young viscacha stirs from sunbathing with a big stretch. It's time to find food, which young viscachas are able to eat as soon as they are born.

A viscacha's view

A day in the life

8:15 am Much of the viscacha's day is spent sunbathing. Exposing its belly to the sunshine, the animal soon warms up after a cold night.

5:30 pm Dusk is the rodent's busiest time, scouring the puna for food. It will eat any plants it finds, including grass and moss.

7:00 pm As night falls, the viscacha heads off to a safe burrow to sleep.

from Condors *to* Cats.

Although they look like rabbits, viscachas are "cousins" of chinchillas.

33

In a land of predators, the puma
is king of the carnivores. It is the
largest cat of the high Andes,
yet it is rarely heard: it doesn't
roar, but has a call that sounds
like a human scream.

A close encounter
Pumas only spend time with others
during mating, or as young cubs with
their mother. The cubs' spotted fur
grows out as they become adults.

Keeping a low profile

The puma's hunting technique is all about surprise. It stays low to the ground, silently stalking the prey, then suddenly springs up and kills its victim with a single, ferocious bite.

A long wait for dinner

7:15 pm A female puma kills a guanaco she has been tracking since dusk. She hunts all day to feed her cubs; now it's time to find food for herself.

7:20 pm There are too many scavengers around for her to eat undisturbed, so the puma drags the carcass into shrubs to hide it until later.

10:00 pm Now that it is dark, the puma finally tucks in. Even though the cubs have eaten during the day, they can't resist a nibble!

1 Spectacled bear

Night is a dangerous time for smaller animals as the darkness brings out some ferocious predators. Pumas and great horned owls can snatch a deer or rodent without warning, while culpeos are expert egg-thieves.

The **vicuñas** have headed back up the slope to their sleeping area just beneath the snowline. They will sleep among the rocks until daybreak.

The **spectacled bear** wanders high into the paramo in its search for food. Mountain-climbing is as easy as scaling a tree for this agile animal.

Young male **culpeos** need to establish their own hunting grounds. Sniffing scent markings tells them if the territory has already been taken.

Mateless **Andean condors** roost in groups at night. There are no nesting materials this high up in the mountains, so the nest is a bare ledge.

The **puma** returns to the prey it buried earlier. It waits until night time to eat, when there are fewer scavengers around to compete for the food.

Named after the white markings on its face, the spectacled bear actually has excellent eyesight.

Since leaving its daytime nest at sunset, the spectacled bear has been foraging in its cloud forest home and up on the paramo. It is more active at night than in the day.

Big bear, small threat
South America's only bear species, the spectacled bear is one of the largest mammals in the Andes. It mostly eats plants, but occasionally tops up its diet with small animals such as rodents.

Despite their size, these bears are very agile. They have no problem shinning up trees or stretching up to the branches for a tasty bromeliad plant.

40

It's twins!

Female bears give birth to two or three tiny cubs that are no bigger than kittens. Home is a den on the forest floor, hidden among rocks or tree roots.

Young cubs can learn essential skills together. A brotherly scrap is good training for adult fighting.

Sharp **claws** are essential tools for tree climbers

After the age of one year, spectacled bears live alone. They are quite timid and are rarely seen.

Swooping

in on an unwary chinchilla, a great horned owl grabs the prey in its talons, killing it instantly. The owl's success is helped by its silent flight.

After eating, owls cough up pellets of the bits of food they do not digest, such as fur and bones.

Soft, loose feathers muffle the sound of flapping wings.

It makes sense
The owl has excellent vision and can see in daylight, but even better at night. It also uses its extraordinary hearing to help it hunt in the dark.

These large tufts are not ears but feathery "horns" that give the owl its name.

Feeding on demand
Great horned owls watch for prey from mountain perches, or while gliding near to the ground. The prey is caught in moments, and the owl rips into it with its bill. Smaller prey is swallowed whole.

The owl's eyes are huge compared to its face. If human eyes were similar, they'd be as big as oranges!

The owl's diet includes rodents, fish, and even other birds, which it plucks before eating.

43

Small animals such as rodents lose heat easily, but the chinchilla braves the freezing night air wrapped in its own fur coat. Each follicle has 60 soft hairs growing from it, making the fur very thick.

A chinchilla has a built-in defence against predators: it moults easily, leaving attackers with a mouthful of fur, not animal. However, it doesn't always work...

The chinchilla's whiskers, or vibrissae, act as an extra pair of eyes at night, when the animal feels its way around in the dark.

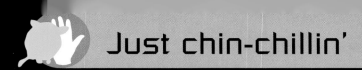
It's been a busy day...

7:00 am Sunning themselves at dawn to get warm and dry, chinchillas start the day with a roll in a dust bath to clean their fur.

3:30 pm Resting in a den among the rocks, a female feeds her kit. Born with a full fur coat, the kit can also eat plants straight from birth.

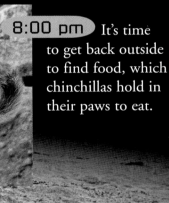

8:00 pm It's time to get back outside to find food, which chinchillas hold in their paws to eat.

Chinchillas are not the only rodents out at night: they share the puna with **montane guinea pigs**. These wild animals are the cousins of the domestic guinea pigs kept as pets all over the world.

Wild guinea pigs live underground in burrows. Their pointed faces are ideally shaped for pushing through tunnels, and also for foraging for plants to eat.

Guinea pigs *live* for about four years in the wild.

Having light-coloured fur is good camouflage for a chinchilla on the rocks.

45

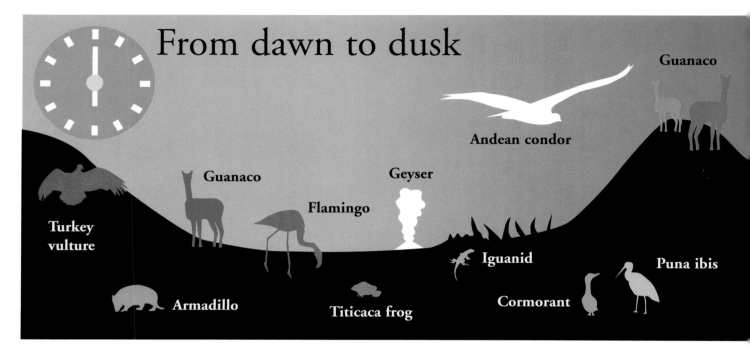

From dawn to dusk

Guanaco

Andean condor

Guanaco

Geyser

Flamingo

Turkey vulture

Iguanid

Puna ibis

Armadillo

Titicaca frog

Cormorant

Glossary

Here are the meanings of some of the important words you will come across as you read about the animals of the mountains.

ALTIPLANO A highland plateau in the central Andes, mostly in Bolivia, but also reaching into Argentina and Chile. It is a region made up of puna and lakes.

CAMOUFLAGE A colour or pattern that blends in with the background, so it can't be seen.

CARCASS The body of a dead animal, especially one that is used for food.

CARNIVORE Animals that eat meat are carnivores.

CLOUD FOREST An evergreen tropical forest found on the lower slopes of mountains. The plants in the forest are surrounded by

COLONY A group of animals of the same species that live together.

DIURNAL Animals that are active during the daytime are diurnal.

FORAGING Grazing for food, particularly plants.

GEYSER A natural pool that shoots a jet of hot water and steam into the air. The pressure and heat for the jet comes from volcanic activity underground.

HERBIVORE Animals that eat only plants are herbivores.

JUVENILE A young animal that is no longer a baby, but is not yet

NOCTURNAL Animals that are active during the night time.

OMNIVORE Animals that eat everything – meat and plants – are omnivores.

PARAMO The lush grasslands of the northern and central Andes. The paramo is near the equator, where it is warm and rainy. As a result, it has more – and bigger – plants than the puna.

PLATEAU A wide, flat area of raised ground. The Altiplano plateau is surrounded by volcanoes.

PREDATOR An animal that hunts, kills, and eats other

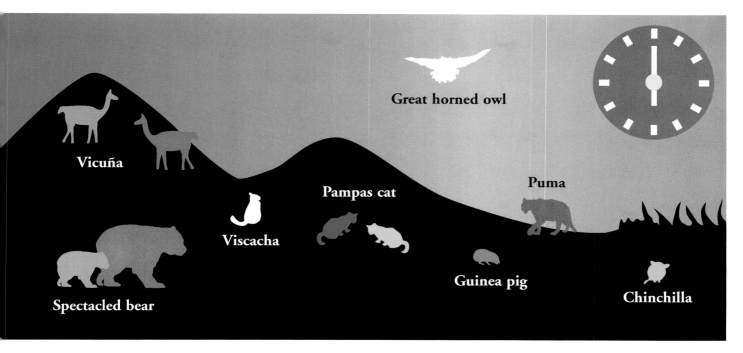

Great horned owl

Vicuña

Pampas cat

Viscacha

Puma

Guinea pig

Spectacled bear

Chinchilla

PREY The animal that is hunted, killed, and eaten by a predator.

PUNA The type of vegetation found in the Altiplano. It is dry and sparse grassland.

ROOST A place where birds perch to sleep or rest. It is also the action of a bird settling down to sleep or rest.

SCAVENGER An animal that looks for carcasses to feed on, rather than hunting for itself.

TALON A bird of prey's sharp, hooked claw, which it uses to catch prey.

THERMAL A current of warm air that rises.

TREE LINE The highest level at which trees can grow. Above the tree line it is too cold for trees.

Picture credits

Index